MADEMOISELLE GRANDS DOIGTS

A CAJUN NEW YEAR'S EVE TALE

Written by Johnette Downing

Illustrated by Heather Stanley

Pelican Publishing Company
GRETNA 2018

ISBN: 9781455623938
Ebook ISBN: 9781455623945

Printed in Malaysia
Published by Pelican Publishing Company, Inc.
1000 Burmaster Street, Gretna, Louisiana 70053

For Miss Isabelle "Flo" Retta for the good gris gris she put on me
to make me write this story—J. D.

For my mother, who loves a good story . . . and shoes—H. S.

In the Cajun Prairie,
where the tall grasses grow,
there is a legend
that all the children know.

Across the bayous and the swamps
in every Acadian home,
one night each year
an old lady will roam.

It started long ago,
or so our fathers tell:
one young maiden
and one evil spell.

Come closer now
as I tell you this tale,
for it happens every New Year's Eve
without fail.

Papa l'An had a daughter
he loved so dear.
He called for her suitors
to come from far and near.

She was generous, her beauty
known across the lands.
**Mademoiselle Grands Doigts
she was called**
for her lovely long fingers and hands.

Young men stood in line like rows of sugarcane.
For acres and acres, they chanted her name.

Each young suitor, with stars in his eyes,
hoped Mademoiselle would be his heart's prize.

They stood in line for hours.
Her hands they wanted to kiss.

**But across Acadiana
something was amiss.**

Like the winds across the prairie,
the news took flight.
Young jealous girls gathered
in the town that night.

They planned a *fais do do*, a party,
but the story gets worse.

They concocted a *gris gris*:
a spell, a curse.

Mademoiselle Grands Doigts,
more radiant than all,
danced with every suitor
who came to the ball.

Her stockings were silk;
her dress was lace.

Her feet in beaded shoes glided the floor with grace.

To accordions and fiddles
she danced every tune.
She smiled and laughed,
making young suitors swoon.

At the end of the night
when the party was through,
Papa l'An and Mademoiselle
bid their hosts adieu.

Back at home
in her moss-filled bed,
she fell into a deep sleep
as she lay down her head.

In the morning, as the sun began to rise,
Mademoiselle Grands Doigts opened her eyes.

Her lovely long fingers were covered in warts
and her hands were ugly and knobby in parts.

Her skin was scaly like a crawfish sack,
and she had bumps on her face and a hump on her back.

Her nose was like a beak of a crane,
and her hair looked like moss
from her bed after rain.

She ran to the attic
never to be seen again,
and to this day,
that is where she has been.

She never got married
   or had children like she dreamed.
The *gris gris* worked
   just as the jealous girls had schemed.

But justice is swift
if nothing at all.

The jealous girls turned green
right after the ball.

Into the swamps they fled,
such a wolfish, horrid sight,
and if you listen closely,
you'll hear them howl at night.

Now I tell it to you
as it was told to me.
Mademoiselle Grands Doigts
still loves children, you see.

On the anniversary of that dance
Papa l'An makes ready
to honor his daughter
with a New Year's Eve party.

Like the stockings and shoes she wore to the ball,
if you put yours out that night,
she will fill them all.

With oranges, gifts, and sweets to delight,
Mademoiselle Grands Doigts blesses all good children
each year on that one and only night.

A Spell of Words

Mademoiselle Grands Doigts
(Mad-mwa-zell Gran Dwa) Young Lady Long Fingers

Madame Grands Doigts
(Madam Gran Dwa) Lady Long Fingers

Papa l'An
(Papa Lan) Father New Year

gris gris
(gree gree) a good or bad spell

fais do do
(fay dough dough) a dance or party

CAJUN NEW YEAR'S EVE
LEGEND

Across Acadiana in Louisiana, the legend of an older Madame Grands Doigts has been passed down orally from one generation to the next. Similar to the tradition of families hanging stockings on Christmas Eve, on New Year's Eve in the Cajun Prairie, families put out their shoes with the hope that Madame Grands Doigts will fill them with oranges, sweets, and small gifts.

Much like the legend of St. Nicholas with his "naughty and nice list," community elders often use the story of Madame to keep children in line. If children misbehave, elders may say, "Madame Grands Doigts will get you with her long, gnarled fingers!" If children behave, elders may say, "Madame Grands Doigts loves good children and she will fill your shoes with treats."

Oral versions of the legend I have heard over the years are too scary for me. Though still somewhat disconcerting, I offer my original written version of the legend, featuring Madame Grands Doigts as a mademoiselle, a young maiden, as a means of preserving this tradition, and to illustrate that one who may appear to be changed on the outside may remain unchanged and true to one's loving and generous nature on the inside.